LAND OF MORNING CALM

KOREAN CULTURE
Then and Now

BY JOHN STICKLER • ILLUSTRATIONS BY SOMA HAN

To former South Korean President Kim Dae Jung
and First Lady Lee Hee Ho.
They dedicated their lives to the future of their people.

Library of Congress Cataloging-in-Publication Data

Stickler, John.
  Land of morning calm : Korean culture then and now / written by John
Stickler ; illustrated by Soma Han Stickler.
      p. cm.
  Summary: Introduces the culture and traditions of Korea, from ancient
times to the present.
  ISBN I-885008-22-8
  I. Korea—History—Juvenile literature. 2.
Korea—Civilization—Juvenile literature. [I. Korea.] I. Stickler, Soma
Han, ill. II. Title.
DS907.4.S75 2003
951.9—dc21

                              2003000285

Printed in China
I0 9 8 7 6 5 4 3 2 I

LAND OF MORNING CALM

KOREAN CULTURE
Then and Now

TABLE OF CONTENTS

CHINA

RUSSIA
Vladivostok

Pyongyang

Ulleungdo

Dokdo

Seoul

KOREA

Pusan

Yellow
Sea

Jejudo

Fukuoka

JAPAN

Shanghai

KOREA: *A Brief Introduction*

THE KOREAN PENINSULA juts southward from the eastern coast of China toward Japan's southern islands. Korea is 85,774 square miles, about the size of Utah or Minnesota. About 70 percent of the terrain is mountainous, and the Korean people live and grow their crops in the rest of the countryside. With four distinct seasons, the weather is similar to New England.

Archeologists have found evidence that people lived on the Korean peninsula in the Stone Age, as far back as 35,000 BC. According to one theory, they migrated all the way from Scandinavia or Finland. Later, waves of immigrants arrived from Turkey, Mongolia, Manchuria and China. Over thousands of years all these people evolved through the Bronze and the Iron Ages and blended into the people we now call Koreans.

The Koreans are a separate race from the Chinese and the Japanese. They have their own distinct language and even look a little different. Koreans are taller than their Asian counterparts, with high foreheads, lighter skin, and higher-bridged noses.

For thousands of years, Korea has been known as *Chosun*, "Land of Morning Calm." Legend has it that the name was given by Korea's mythical founder, Dan-gun, who was enchanted by the peaceful dawn.

Korea was unified into one nation in the 7th century, and it has remained an independent country ruled by a series of Korean kings and queens. Although it was invaded numerous times — by Japanese, Mongolian, and Chinese armies — Korea has always recovered its independence.

While China and Japan were developing trade with Western countries in the 19th century, Korea kept its doors closed, even fighting off visiting foreign ships. Korea became known as The Hermit Kingdom because of this attitude.

At the beginning of the Cold War in 1945, Korea was divided at the 38th parallel with American troops stationed to the south and Soviet Union forces to the north. The two military powers were assigned to keep order on the peninsula while Korea prepared for its first democratic election. On June 25, 1950 the North Korean army, with Soviet approval, invaded South Korea. Once again Korea became a battleground.

United Nations military units from 16 countries came to the aid of the South, battling North Korean and Communist Chinese armies for three long years. When the fighting ended in 1953, millions of people had died, the cities had been reduced to rubble, and the country had been destroyed.

Ten years later, Korea initiated a series of five-year economic development plans. Industries, manufacturing, and exports developed rapidly and the hardworking Koreans launched a phenomenal growth period unmatched by any country in history.

By the end of the 20th century, South Korea had risen from a war-destroyed economy to the 11th largest economic power in the world.

Korea is still divided today. In 1991 the United Nations recognized the Communist North and the Democratic South as two separate countries. Kim Dae Jung was elected president of South Korea in 1997 and pledged to re-establish contact between the two halves of the country, deadly enemies for half a century. His peaceful "Sunshine Policy" led to an unprecedented summit meeting. In June 2000, President Kim went to Pyongyang, the capital of North Korea, for talks with his Communist counterpart and received the 2000 Nobel Peace Prize for his efforts.

The chances that North and South Korea will be reunited like East and West Germany are complicated by tensions between North Korea and the world. The United States and neighboring countries like Japan, China and Russia are concerned that North Korea may make a nuclear bomb. Until these tensions are resolved, the world's eyes will be on the Korean peninsula for some time to come.

단 군

The Myth of Dan-gun: KOREA'S BEGINNINGS

EVERY KOREAN KNOWS that their country was founded in 2333 B.C. — the legend is very clear about that!

The story goes like this: thousands of years ago, a divine being named Hwan-un descended from Heaven to teach the primitive people of Korea. He taught them 360 basic skills including agriculture, medicine, carpentry, weaving and fishing – everything they needed to build a society.

At that time a bear and a tiger were living in a cave on Mount Taebaek. Both of them wished to become human beings and prayed to Hwan-un daily. Hwan-un took pity on them and decided to help, calling them to him and gaving them 100 bulbs of garlic.

"Eat all of this garlic," he said, "and stay inside your cave for 100 days without leaving. After 100 days, you will have your wish." The tiger and the bear went into their cave and began eating the garlic. The tiger soon became restless and came out to get some sunshine. The bear was patient and stayed inside for the full 100 days. Lo and behold, the bear emerged as a beautiful woman, known as Ungnyo.

Ungnyo married Hwan-un and the following year, 2333 B.C., they had a son named Dan-gun.

When Dan-gun grew up, he became the first human king of the Korean peninsula. He established his capital in Pyongyang, now in North Korea, and called his kingdom *Chosun,* "Land of Morning Calm." He must have inherited some divine powers of his own because, according to the legend, he ruled the country for the next 1,500 years.

After his long reign he stepped down from the throne to become a mountain spirit, with a wild tiger as his messenger. 🔲

Dan-gun, the mythical founder of Korea.

Taekuk:
THE KOREAN FLAG

태극기

IN 1872, KING KOJONG of Korea sent two royal representatives to Japan to discuss the relationship between the two countries. For over 2000 years, the kingdom of Korea had flown military banners in battle on land or sea but had no official national flag. On this trip to Japan, the two diplomats carried with them their country's first, brand new flag.

This original flag may seem simple, but parts of the design have many interpretations. The white background could represent the land of Korea, the Confucian symbol of purity, or the Buddhist concept of 'emptiness'. The circular symbol in the center represents the people of Korea, while the three lines in each corner stand for the royal government.

The round red-and-blue yin-yang symbol traditionally represents the eternal balance of the universe or harmony between opposites. The red half on top is yang and it represents things like heaven, day, male, heat and action. The blue yin on the bottom represents things like earth, night, female, cold and passive.

The black three-line symbols, called trigrams, are from the *Chu Yok*, known in the West as the *I Ching* or the mystical Book of Changes. There are eight possible three-line combinations using solid and broken lines. (Can you figure out the other four?) Each combination has a name and a symbolic meaning given by the Chinese more than four thousand years ago. ▨

THE FLAG'S SYMBOLS

"Force" represents heaven, persist, sovereign, <u>struggle</u>, enduring

"Gorge" means water, north, black and "<u>dangerous</u> place"

"Radiance" for fire, south and "envisioning <u>common goals</u>"

"Field" for mother earth, yield, "ground on which human world rests"

The simplest meanings of the four trigrams on the flag are Heaven, Earth, Fire and Water. But some of the secondary meanings, Struggle, Danger, and Common Goals, reveal how nervous King Kojong's diplomats were when they sailed to Japan to meet their age-old enemies. The four corner symbols express both the caution and the hope in their hearts for the common future of the two nations.

King Kojong introduced the new flag to his subjects with this basic interpretation, although it was later modified slightly to the format we see today.

Sadly, the new flag was taken down in 1910 when Japan occupied Korea. It was not raised proudly over Korean soil again until the end of World War Two in 1945. ▨

호랑이

Horangi: THE TIGER

CAN YOU IMAGINE living with wild tigers nearby? In olden days, tigers, or *horangi*, inhabited the wooded mountains of Korea. Farmers and rural folk lived with this danger all around them. They had to worry about their pigs, their chickens, and even themselves. Fear and respect for the tiger was well founded and only the bravest of men would go out to hunt the *horangi*. The king even kept a tiger skin as a rug in front of his throne to impress visitors.

Over the centuries the myth and mystery of the tiger grew far beyond the reality of the striped hunter in the hills. Despite its danger to people, Koreans adopted the tiger as a symbol of protection and here the real tiger blurs and blends with the mythical tiger. The tiger and the dragon were considered equal and were both seen as protective forces. High on the central wooden roof beam, or *daedulpo*, of every

The white tiger and blue dragon: protection and strength.

Korean house, one could find the carved Chinese characters for 'dragon' at one end and 'tiger' at the other.

In January, each household would tack a paper painting of a tiger or dragon up on the inner gate of the house to scare away evil spirits and protect the residents against misfortune in the coming year. Many Koreans carried small, hand-painted, or embroidered tiger amulets in their pocket or purse for "protection" wherever they went.

White Tiger and Blue Dragon

For centuries the tiger has also been associated with the military. Korean fighting units admired the fierce feline and adorned their banners and uniforms with its image. When South Korea sent two Army divisions to Southeast Asia during the Vietnam War, they fought beneath the banners of the White Tiger and the Blue Dragon.

Gradually the fearless animal grew to represent Korea and its people. Although not one of the giant cats has been seen in the country for nearly a hundred years, the *horangi* has become a symbol of the nation itself, much like the eagle is to America.

When Korea hosted the 1988 Olympics, officials naturally selected a tiger image as mascot of the 24th Games. The cute figure was called *Hodori*, or "Tiger Boy." 🔲

THE PERSIMMON TREE 감나무

Persimmon tree in the Fall.

THE PERSIMMON TREE is unusual because when its big leaves drop off in the fall, the bright orange fruit is left hanging from the bare branches. Almost every house in a Korean village had a persimmon tree in the yard. In November, when cold winds blow and the landscape is dull and dreary, the bright spots of color lift the heart.

According to rural tradition the persimmon tree is deeply respected for its "seven excellences":

> it lives an exceptionally long time
> it provides generous shade
> no birds will nest in the branches
> the wood is free of grubs and insects
> its branches are particularly beautiful after the first frost
> it bears fine fruit, delicious fresh or dried
> its large leaves may be used for writing on

One could add an eighth excellent attribute: the wood of the persimmon tree makes beautiful furniture. When cut and polished, the wood is an unusual orange and black color, like Halloween stripes. An antique Korean chest, with panels of persimmon wood, is considered a treasure in the home.

Even today, persimmon fruit is appreciated for its beauty, unique taste, and nutrition. A box of freshly picked persimmons makes an impressive gift when calling on friends. *Kokam*, dried persimmons that are flattened and strung together on a string, provide sweet desserts all winter without refrigeration.

Wherever they are, Koreans carry a special love for the persimmon tree, as if it were a living symbol of their country. ▨

Folktale:

A HUNGRY TIGER, looking for something (or someone) to eat, crept into a Korean village just after sundown. Hiding outside a thatch-roof house, he could hear voices inside. A little boy was crying and his mother was trying to quiet him. "If you don't stop crying," she warned, "a hungry tiger will take you and eat you up."

The tiger listened, expecting the child to quiet down. But no, he kept on bawling. "Wow," the tiger thought, "this boy is not afraid of anything."

The mother continued to plead with her son, "You better stop crying. I'll get the *kokam*." Suddenly the crying stopped.

"Uh-oh," the tiger thought. "The boy's not afraid of me, but he's terrified of this *kokam*. Whatever it is, it must be bigger and tougher than me!"

And he slunk away into the night.

한글 Hangul: THE KOREAN ALPHABET

DURING THE CHOSUN Dynasty, the people of Korea spoke their own language but wrote using Chinese characters. This was awkward because Chinese is not suitable for writing Korean properly. And since the Chinese ideographs are so difficult to learn, only a small percentage of the population was educated enough to read and write.

An enlightened ruler known today as King Sejong the Great was concerned about illiteracy among his subjects. He ordered his wise men to develop a basic alphabet that would be easy to learn. These court-appointed scholars produced a set of 28 symbols, creating one of the simplest alphabets in the world, *Hangul*.

In 1446, King Sejong introduced the new alphabet and decreed that his people should now learn to read, write and communicate in print. That announcement, called the **hunmin chong-um** ("correct sounds to teach the people"), was distributed nationwide and was the very first text printed in Hangul. In his proclamation the King wrote:

The sounds of our language differ from those of Chinese and are not easily communicated using Chinese ideographs. Therefore, many are among the ignorant. Though they wish to express their sentiments in writing, they have been unable to communicate. Considering this situation with compassion, I have newly devised twenty-eight letters. I wish only that the people will learn them easily and use them conveniently in their daily life.

King Sejong

CONSONANTS

ㄱ	ㄴ	ㄷ	ㄹ	ㅁ	ㅂ	ㅅ
k, g	n	t, d	r, l	m	p, b	s, sh

ㅇ	ㅈ	ㅊ	ㅋ	ㅌ	ㅍ	ㅎ
ng	ch, j	ch'	k'	t'	p'	h

VOWELS

ㅏ	ㅑ	ㅓ	ㅕ	ㅗ
a	ya	ŏ	yŏ	o

ㅛ	ㅜ	ㅠ	ㅡ	ㅣ
yo	u	yu	ŭ	i

The new system of Korean writing was promoted nationally while King Sejong was alive, but after his death it wasn't used as much.

It wasn't until the end of the 19th century that *Hangul* was revived. When "The Hermit Kingdom" opened its doors to the West eager American missionaries wanted to introduce Christian texts to the Korean people. They needed a written language, so *Hangul* was promptly put to use to translate the Bible into Korean.

By then, the 400-year-old alphabet had been neglected for so long that everyone remembered it differently. A special conference convened in 1933 to address the issue and *Hangul* was trimmed and standardized. The original 28 letters were cut to 24 — 14 consonants and 10 vowels, and put in a clear, phonetic format. The alphabet Koreans use today is the result of that meeting.

The alphabet is so easy to learn that today virtually everyone in the country can read. Korea enjoys one of the highest literacy rates in the world. 🔲

MOVABLE TYPE

KOREANS WERE USING movable type as early as 1234 A.D., decades before Gutenberg developed the process in Germany. At that time, all printing in Korea was done with Chinese characters — carved of wood, ceramic, or cast in metal. After 1446, King Sejong ordered the casting of printing type in his new alphabet to publish books in *Hangul* as well as Chinese characters. 🔲

도장 *Dojang:* STAMPING YOUR SIGNATURE

FOR CENTURIES, KOREANS have pressed a carved seal dipped in red ink onto important documents instead of signing their names. The resulting red mark, usually the person's name spelled in Chinese characters, became his or her official "signature." The Korean word for this handy seal is *dojang*.

As with so much of Korea's culture, the idea for the *dojang* came from China where the seal was called a chop. A document wasn't official until it was "chopped" by someone with authority. A writer would put his red seal at the end of a letter to prove it really was from him. Europeans used seals for centuries, except they would press theirs into hot wax on the outside of the letter, both to indicate it was authentic and to show the recipient that the envelope had not been opened.

The head of every household had a *dojang* for "signing" letters, opening bank accounts, and confirming documents such as the ownership deed to his house. This made the *dojang* very precious, for if someone stole the registered seal he could sell the house without the owner's permission and keep the money! The *dojang* was always kept in a very safe place.

The King's Seal

The Korean king had a royal seal for stamping official state documents. In old Korea the king was the legal authority, and his seal on a royal decree meant it was the law of the land. The king's chop was not called a *dojang* – it was much too important for that. It was called an *oak-sae* and it was heavy and impressive, carved from some precious stone like jade. When the king pressed his *oak-sae* onto a royal document, it meant business!

In 1882, the United States was given permission to open one of its first foreign embassies on the Korean peninsula. The historic diplomatic agreement was "signed" with the king's *oak-sae*.

Unique Designs

What does a *dojang* look like? Often it depends on the owner. *Dojangs* can be cylindrical or square, long or short, fat or thin. In the old days, a rich man would have his carved out of ivory — pure white, smooth and elegant. He kept it in a little pouch made of silk, velvet, or perhaps soft leather. Other fancy *dojangs* were carved from jade, amber, fine marble or deer horn. The average man would have a wooden *dojang*. Not only is wood inexpensive, but it is also much easier to carve.

Each *dojang* seal is custom-carved for the owner, so no two are identical. For one thing, the family name may be carved in Chinese or Korean characters. Or a woman may carry a seal with a script that looks more feminine. And if you want something really different, specialty carvers can create an artistic design following ancient mystical principles, bringing the owner good luck.

Legend says that a *dojang* carved from the wood of a tree struck by lightning will protect the owner from danger. Why? Because lightning never strikes twice!

The Dojang Today

Use of the hand seal has not faded into Korea's cultural history. Modern offices in Korea still depend on "chops" to keep paperwork moving through the bureaucracy. Each red mark on the document indicates another level of approval. Today most seals are made of plastic and have a tight-fitting plastic cap, instead of a leather pouch, to keep the red ink from smudging things. It is not unusual to see a modern Korean office supply catalog selling electric staplers, cell phones—and *dojangs*.

King Yi Tae Jo, founder of the Second Chosun Dynasty

종교 RELIGIOUS BELIEFS THROUGH THE YEARS

A gold-plated bronze statue of a Boddhisatva, an enlightened teacher of Buddhism. Cast in Korea around 600 A.D.

FOR MANY CENTURIES, three belief systems existed side by side in Korea: Animism, Confucianism, and Buddhism. A person could practice one, two, or all three at the same time. Later, when Christianity came to Korea, peoples' beliefs were shared among the four religions.

Animism

The earliest religion in Korea was the spirit worship called Animism. Animism has no churches, priests or bible. People who practice Animism believe that everything — mountains, trees, animals — has a spirit and that they should live in harmony with these spirits. Ceremonies were held to ask for a good harvest, to start the New Year with prosperity and good health, or to call for rain in a drought.

The *mudang* was a special shaman or sorceress who communicated with the invisible spirit world. Animism and shamans have always existed in Korea, from before Korean history was even recorded up to this very day.

Confucianism

Confucianism may not actually be a religion since it doesn't deal with what happens when you die, and there are no churches. It is more like a moral system that teaches people how to relate to each other and how to be good. Confucius was a wise man who lived in China from 550-478 B.C. He taught his followers to obey their parents, pay respect to their ancestors, and be nice to their neighbors. His strict moral rules for individuals, families, and the structure of governments were supposed to make society stable and peaceful.

Education is very important to Confucianism, and the National Confucian College was established during the Silla Dynasty in 682. Today, one of the leading colleges in Seoul is Sungkyunkwan University, a Confucian school founded in 1411.

Buddhism

Buddhism is very popular in Korea and was the official state religion for more than 800 years. It teaches that by meditating and living a simple, pure life, one can achieve enlightenment.

Buddhism is considered a true religion with temples, monasteries, monks, nuns, and 320,000 pages of scripture.

Originally from India, Buddhism was introduced into China in the second century B.C. The first Buddhist monk to arrive in Korea, a Chinese man named Shun-tao, came in 372 A.D. with a letter of introduction from the Chinese king of Eastern Chin. The monk's mission to spread the beliefs was very successful and by 528 A.D. Buddhism was declared the official state religion of Korea.

Christianity

The fourth and newest religion in Korea is Christianity. This religion is exclusive and teaches that if you want to be a Christian, you cannot be a Confucian, a Buddhist or an Animist. Even so, it has become very popular in Korea.

The first Christian missionary to enter Korea came from China in 1686, probably a Chinese priest of the Roman Catholic faith. During the century afterward, many Koreans chose to become Catholics, but the king and the royal court were very suspicious of the new religion. They considered it a dangerous kind of foreign invasion.

The royal court soon outlawed Christianity and even executed some of the new Korean Catholics, but the religion still continued to grow. In 1837, three French priests sneaked into the country to preach to the converts. One of these missionaries was the first Bishop of Korea, assigned to The Hermit Kingdom by the Pope himself. All three were arrested by the Korean government and ordered to leave the country. When they refused, they were declared traitors and executed.

This type of suppression continued until the 1880s when treaties signed with European countries and the United States allowed Christian missionaries to live in Korea, practicing and teaching their faith. Today, approximately 50 percent of Korea's population follows some religious faith. Of these, about 46 percent are Buddhists, 39 percent are Protestants, and 13 percent are Catholics. ▨

A Buddhist nun strolls on the grounds of Pulguksa Temple in Kyongju.

휴일 CELEBRATIONS!

HOW MANY HOLIDAYS do you celebrate every year? In olden days, Koreans observed a holiday nearly every month of the lunar calendar. This is the calendar based on the monthly cycle of the moon instead of the sun. Each month begins with the new moon, and the months don't always coincide with the months on the solar calendar we use now.

Some holidays were merely special days set aside for paying respect to one's ancestors, while others had a much greater importance to all Koreans. Those are the holidays that are still celebrated around the country today.

Lunar Calendar Holidays

The first lunar holiday every year is, of course, New Year's Day. On our more familiar solar calendar, the actual date of the Lunar New Year changes from year to year but always falls sometime between January 21 and February 20. To celebrate the Lunar New Year, everyone dresses up in their finest traditional clothes and goes around to visit relatives and friends. Young children bow deeply, or *saebae*, to their parents and grandparents and receive a small gift in return.

The most popular New Year's game is *yut-nori* (*nori* means 'game'). Children and grownups play it on a board like Monopoly, except they roll four half-round sticks instead of dice. Players move their pieces around the board according to the numbers thrown and the team that reaches the end first is the winner. With a lucky throw you can knock your opponent off the board so that they have to start all over. Believe it or not, a *yut* game can get pretty loud and rowdy.

Outdoors on New Year's Day, girls jump up and down on a type of seesaw called a *nultwigi*. The men and boys fly little square kites made of rice paper and thin bamboo strips. They say that you can write your worries and fears on the kite and let it fly out to the end of the string. When the kite is as high as it can go, you cut the string and watch all your troubles float away on the wind.

Some men make special fighting kites, their strings coated with ground glass. A talented kite fighter can cut the string of his opponent's kite by skillfully maneuvering his kite through the sky.

Korea barely recovers from that holiday when a second January festival arrives, *Daeborum* (Biggest Moon of the Year). It always falls on January 15th by the lunar calendar because the moon is always full at

16

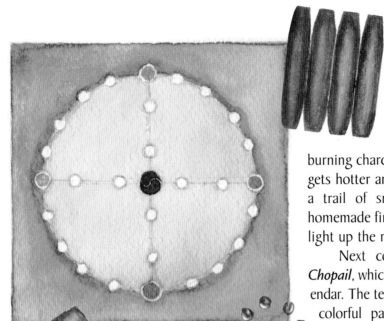

the middle of the month. Farmers in the country burn the dry grass around the rice paddies at night to kill the bugs, and they greet the full moon by swinging buckets of burning charcoal at the end of a rope. The coal gets hotter and hotter as it spins, throwing off a trail of snapping, white-hot sparks. Like homemade fireworks, the spinning, fiery circles light up the night sky.

Next comes Buddha's Birthday, *Sawol Chopail*, which falls on April 8th of the lunar calendar. The temples are hung with colorful paper lanterns and faithful Buddhists come from miles around to light incense and honor the ancient prophet from India.

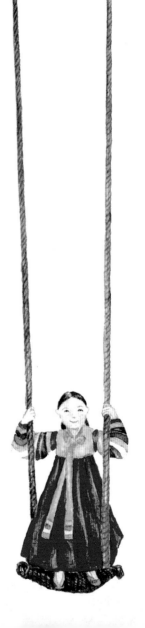

May 5th is *Dano*, celebrating the arrival of summer. Daring girls in colorful *hanbok* dresses swing standing up, higher and higher, on special tall swings (*guneh*) with very long ropes.

Chusok, the annual Harvest Festival, falls on the day of a full moon, always August 15th by the lunar calendar. Families prepare "moon cakes," tasty rice cakes steamed on pine needles. Farmers and city folk alike celebrate the rice harvest and visit the hillside graves of their ancestors to pay their respects, an old Confucian custom. Afterward they enjoy a picnic on the grass.

In the villages, troupes of gaily-dressed dancers parade to every house, twirling streamers attached to their hats and dancing to the joyous sound of gongs and drums.

Solar Calendar Holidays

By combining Western and Eastern customs, Koreans get to celebrate two New Year's Days. The solar January 1st is a national holiday, as it is around the world. Banks and businesses close as the people say farewell to the old year and welcome in the fresh new one. Then, about a month later, they observe the lunar New Year for several days.

Eight other solar dates are also national holidays in Korea, including the two biggest celebrations: Liberation Day and Christmas Day. Liberation Day in Korea is like Independence Day in the United States. It falls on August 15th because on that day in 1945, Korea gained its freedom from Japanese occupation at the end of World War Two. And although Christmas is a Christian holiday, most Koreans, Christian or not, celebrate on December 25 by exchanging gifts and enjoying festive family gatherings.

한국음식 TIME TO EAT

A KOREAN MEAL traditionally consists of rice, soup, *kimchi* (a kind of pickle) and many little side dishes called *banchan*. The side dishes offer a variety of tastes and textures including seafood, meats, soybean curd (*tubu*) and many different vegetables. Each meal would have a dozen or more different *banchan* that provided all the nutrients for a complete meal. Not only were the dishes good for you, they were beautiful to look at, too. There were usually foods of five different colors on the table — red, green, yellow, white and black — representing the five elements: fire, wood, earth, metal and water.

Kimchi

In old Korea, before the days of refrigerators and supermarkets, people needed a way to keep vegetables and fruits through the cold winter. Drying preserved some fruits and vegetables, and pickling was another solution. Koreans pickled cabbages and turnips, which were served throughout the winter to provide much-needed nutrients. Korea's unique pickled cabbage is called *kimchi*.

How do you make *kimchi*? Long Chinese cabbages are first soaked in salt water as a preservative. Then the cabbages are rinsed with clean water and stuffed with mashed garlic, green onion, ginger, and lots of hot red pepper flakes. The exact recipes for *kimchi* vary from region to region and household to household. Some families add items such as anchovies or pickled fish, fruits, or nuts to make it taste even better.

After soaking, the cabbage is packed into huge brown ceramic jars, "*kimchi* pots," and buried in the back yard with just the open top sticking above the ground. It is covered with a matching brown ceramic lid and protected from the cold with rice straw.

As the ground freezes, a thin layer of ice may form in the pot, but the vegetables stay crunchy and "fresh" all winter long. As the months pass, the marinating mixture slowly ferments, adding a tangy flavor like German sauerkraut.

Every November, families and neighbors gathered for the making of *kimchi*, a major kitchen event of the year and a festive and joyful task. One household might have purchased 100 cabbages, enough to last a large family through the winter, and the pickling project could take several days.

Kimchi can be made from many other things beside cabbages, like cucumbers, mustard greens, or the big white turnips Koreans call *mu*.

Today, of course, many people have no room for 100 cabbages and no backyard to bury *kimchi* pots. But with greenhouses, express shipping, and supermarkets, fresh fruits and vegetables are available all year round anyway.

These days *kimchi* is always available in the market, ready-made in modern factories. It has become a global food as well, exported to *kimchi*-lovers in countries around the world. ▨

Buddhist temple foods

Traditionally, Buddhist nuns and monks lived on a special diet. They did not eat meat or use "the five strong-flavored ingredients" in their food. So temple recipes never included hot pepper, garlic, leeks, wild green onions or ginger. Instead they dined on wild mountain vegetables, garden greens, edible roots and bark, berries, seaweeds, nuts, and grains for a mild and healthful menu.

Today these recipes are gaining popularity and can be found in special "temple food" restaurants around Korea or served to visitors at some Buddhist temples in the mountains. ▨

음악 MUSIC

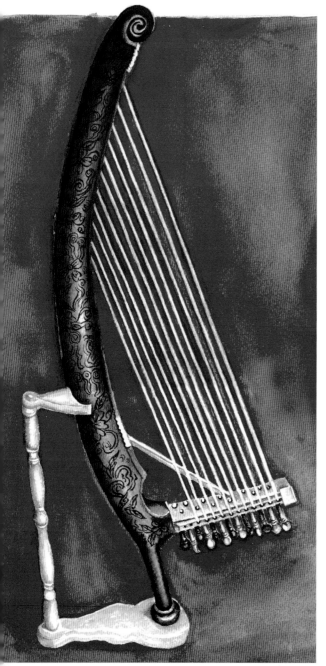

The sogonghu, a vertical harp from the 2nd century B.C.

KOREANS HAVE ALWAYS loved music. The common people had their folk music, with simple melodies and only a few basic instruments, while the royal court had more formal and complex compositions known as *hyang-ak*.

Folk songs, farmers' music and story-singing, *pansori*, were usually accompanied by drums, gongs, and a simple bamboo flute called a *piri.*. But in ancient times there was only a single metal wind instrument called the *napal*, a long, trumpet-like horn that sounded just one, low note. Imagine making music with only one note!

Koreans say their folk music appeals to the senses, while *hyang-ak* appeals to the soul. Royal court music was performed by an orchestra with many wind and stringed instruments. The stringed instruments looked like either harps or lutes. The main Korean string instrument, in use for over a thousand years, is a kind of horizontal harp called a *gayageum*. Unlike any Western instrument, it lies flat on the floor and is plucked by a musician kneeling next to it. The *gayageum* has 12 strings, but later versions have 15 or 25 strings.

Drums are an important part of all folk and royal Korean music. Big drums, called *changgo*, hang from wooden stands and boom dramatically when struck. Folk musicians play a drum shaped like an hourglass with drumheads at each end. The player carries the drum by a strap over the shoulder and marches or dances while beating out a staccato rhythm. One unusual old instrument still seen in Confucian ceremonies has 16 L-shaped polished stone slabs, hung from a frame with strings. Musicians in ancient costumes strike these heavy chimes with a hammer made of ox horn. During the Chosun Dynasty, King Sejong ordered one of his scholars to revise the court music to make it more Korean and less Chinese. He also had new musical instruments developed and new compositions commissioned for his royal court.

When Japan's ruler Hideyoshi sent an army to conquer Korea in the 16th century, many of the *hyang-ak* musicians were killed or kidnapped. The performance of royal court music diminished for decades, but eventually people resumed playing music. Today the Korean National Classical Music Institute keeps the ancient art form alive. Western music is also alive and well in Korea. American missionaries introduced their church music into the country at the end of the 19th century, and after World War Two all forms of Western music flooded in. Classical music became instantly popular and the Korea Philharmonic Orchestra Society was established in 1945. The National Opera House stands proudly on a hill overlooking the capital of Seoul.

When rock-and-roll first arrived in Seoul in the 1960s, the authorities condemned it as "Western decadence." Boys who grew their hair long like the Beatles were rounded up by police and given instant haircuts! 🀧

Changgo *drum, an integral part of all Korean music.*

Dance: Formality and Fun

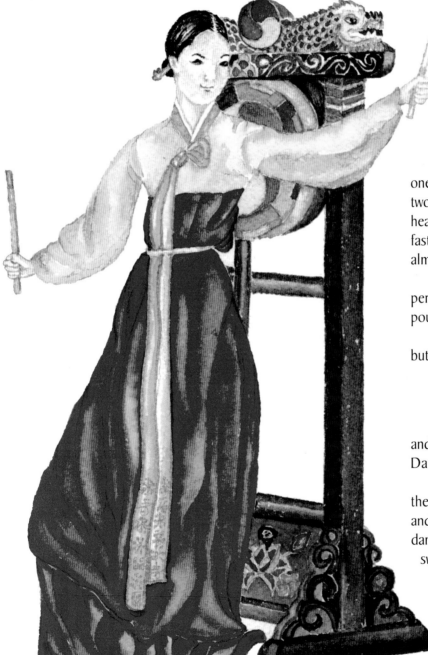

WHAT KIND OF DANCING do you like? It's probably very different from the traditional dances of Korea.

Court Dances

Through the dynasties, dance performances in Korea's royal court were always quite formal. Most of them were slow and stately, performed by women in beautiful silk costumes.

A lovely young woman, dressed in a flowing gown, performs one of the most dramatic of the court dances, the Drum Dance. With two sticks in hand she gradually approaches a large drum mounted head-high on a colorful stand. Slowly at first, one beat at a time, then faster and faster, her drumming builds steadily into an intense and almost hypnotizing performance.

Today, this enthralling exhibition is still very popular and may be performed by three or more highly skilled drummers clicking and pounding their sticks in unison.

According to royal records there were 56 official court dances but only a few of them are still known or performed today.

Folk Dances

Folk dances of the common people were usually held outdoors, and two of the most popular were the Farmers' Dance and the Mask Dance.

In rural villages, farmers would celebrate the fall rice harvest and the spring rice planting with ritual dances accompanied by drumming and the clanging of gongs. During the Farmers' Dance, a man would dance with a long streamer or wide ribbon attached to his hat. By swinging his head just right he could keep the long ribbon whirling around him, like a cowboy with a lasso.

The Mask Dances were like life-size puppet shows with actors in carved wooden masks playing the roles of various villagers. They could act silly and stupid, making everyone laugh. Long before the arrival of television, these humorous plays were performed outdoors with songs and narration.

During the Japanese occupation from 1910-1945, no Korean dancing was allowed. Since then, the old arts have been rediscovered and encouraged in order to save, and savor, Korea's cultural heritage. Today, these traditional dances as well as most forms of Western and modern dance are enjoyed by everyone.

In the 1980s the Korean government decreed some ancient dances as "Intangible Cultural Properties," including *Cheoyongmu,* the Mask Dance of the Silla Dynasty, *Hangmu*, the Crane Dance of the Koryo Dynasty, and *Chunaengjeon*, the Nightingale-Singing-in-the-Spring dance of the Chosun Dynasty. The professional performers who revived these dances were designated "Human Cultural Assets," the highest honor awarded to masters of traditional arts and crafts. ▨

23

Hanbok: Traditional Fashions

If Koreans want to feel more Korean, all they have to do is put on their *hanbok*.

The Korean word for their traditional costume is *hanbok*, and it refers to both men's and women's clothing. The *hanbok* is quite distinctive from other Asian styles.

Long influenced by Chinese fashions, Korean women used to wear long, full trousers and hip-length jackets. After the Mongol invasion in the 13th century, the jacket was shortened and women wore full, ankle-length skirts called *chima* fastened high on the waist.

In the 15th century women's styles changed again. The skirt became fuller and was raised up much further to tie right under the arms. The jacket, or *chogori*, was shortened even more. This traditional costume has been modernized many times and many ways — with elegant fabrics, colors, embroidery and accessories – but the basic dress remains much the same as it was in 1500.

During the Chosun Dynasty (1392-1910) the Confucian royal court introduced some new costumes. For example, brides began to wear a special robe over their wedding *chima* and *chogori*. It was called a *wonsam* and was made of flowing green satin or silk with a red lining that you could see from the open sides. The wide sleeves were striped in red, yellow, pink, green and blue. At weddings today, brides may still be seen wearing the traditional finery introduced centuries ago.

Chosun Dynasty tradition dictated that young girls

should wear yellow jackets and bright red skirts. Once they were married, women would wear green jackets and red skirts instead. Today, of course, women wear any color or fabric they want. Older women still prefer to wear *hanbok*, although in more subdued colors and patterns. Parents like to dress their children in bright-colored *chogori* with rainbow-striped sleeves.

High-fashion *hanbok* are still popular for special occasions such as holidays, weddings and parties. Clothes are made of silk brocade or satin for winter, and lighter fabrics, including silks, for warmer seasons. In summer, hand-woven ramie cloth, a natural fiber, is sewn into cool, heavily starched garments.

The curved sleeves, narrow white collar, and long, graceful bow on the front of the woman's jacket emphasizes the beauty of the traditional *hanbok* costume. It is said that the full, curving sleeve was inspired by the luminous half-moon in the night sky.

The Korean *hanbok* is usually decorated with accessories like colorful silk purses (*pokjumoni*), or an ornamental pendant (*norigae*) hanging under the bow of the jacket. The *norigae* is often a carved piece of jade, silver or gold, with a long, silk tassel attached.

These days, most Koreans wear Western clothing in the cities – suits and ties for businessmen and dresses, suits or skirts-and-blouses for women. ▦

다듬이

Dademi:
IRONING WITH STICKS AND STONES

THESE DAYS, WE iron our clothes with electric irons. But how did Koreans keep their clothes pressed shiny and flat in the days before electricity?

They used a system unique to Korea and Japan that involved a long, smooth stone and two rounded wooden bats or paddles. Winter woolens would be drip-dried and then pressed onto the stone. One woman, or two together, would pound on the material with their little bats until it was flattened and wrinkle free.

The same system was used for clothing and sheets, but starch made of rice flour and water would be applied before the pounding began. The rice flour starch made the cloth stiff and smooth and the fabric would rustle whenever the wearer walked.

This process of ironing was called *dademi* and the stone platform was a *dademi-dol* (*dol* means 'stone'). The *dademi-dol* ironing boards were usually carved out of marble or other smooth stone, but some were made of polished hardwood. Fancy ones had carved legs, inscriptions, little sculptures, or folk paintings on them. The wooden bats used for pounding were called *bangmengi*.

Usually the mother in the household would pound the laundry with her daughter-in-law. The steady rhythm of four bats beating cloth on stone created a kind of cheerful, household percussion music.

Sometimes, the father of the bride, visiting his daughter for the first time at her new home, would bring her a *dademi-dol* as a marriage gift. It was more than a useful home "appliance," it was also an instrument for the daughter to work off her stress. Korean mothers-in-law were known to be very tough on their sons' wives, who had to obey their every order.

Every Korean household had one or more *daedemi-dol*, but with the introduction of electricity the old custom began fading away. Now, instead of the hollow toka-toka-toka of *bangmengi* echoing wordless stories through the darkened village, one hears the chatter of many television sets. The only *dademi-dol* you will find today are in museums. ◈

태권도

Taekwondo:
KOREA'S UNIQUE MARTIAL ART

CHINA HAS KUNG FU. Japan has karate. Korea's martial art is called *taekwondo*. It is a form of unarmed self-defense, fighting that emphasizes the strength of the legs and feet in addition to strong arm blows.

Have you see pictures of a man breaking a stack of bricks with his hand? Or splitting a wooden board with a flying side-kick? That is probably someone demonstrating the personal power of *taekwondo*. Over the years, the fighting technique has developed into a popular form of exercise and a competitive sport practiced by people of all ages, from pre-school children to middle-aged men and women.

Taekwondo is popular because it so effectively develops self-discipline, mental concentration, and physical fitness. The student begins by mastering basic poses and arm and leg exercises. Building strength and coordination, he or she moves up through the various skill levels indicated by a different colored belt worn around the white, buttonless uniform. Beginning students wear a white belt. *Taekwondo* masters at the top levels wear a black belt.

Archeological evidence from caves and tombs shows that *taekwondo* has been practiced in Korea for about 2,000 years. During the Shilla Dynasty (57 B.C. – 935 A.D.) an educational institution was developed for promising young men. This elite youth corps was called *hwarang-do* and it was devoted to studies and martial arts. Ancient documents tell us that in their training the young men practiced *taekwondo*.

In 1973 the World Taekwondo Federation was founded in Seoul. Today some 3.8 million Koreans belong to the Taekwondo Association and worldwide, more than 30 million people in 140 countries enjoy the sport.

Taekwondo was introduced as a regular event at the Tenth Asian Games and was a demonstration event at the 1988 Summer Olympics in Seoul. At the 2000 Summer Olympics in Sydney, Australia it became a full medal sport and a recognized Olympic event.

Statue of Warrior "Kumgang" in Sok Guram Cave in Gyung ju

도자기 CERAMICS: TREASURES OF CLAY

CLAY POTTERY IS EASY TO BREAK.

Most of Korea's early ceramic art was destroyed over centuries of wars, invasions and normal wear and tear. Many of the remaining pieces from the last 2,000 years survived only because they were buried safely underground. We can thank the early kings and queens for their custom of stocking their tombs with ceramic containers of food and other things they might need on their journey to heaven! Much of the antique pottery that you can see today in museums was dug up from royal tombs only recently.

Most precious are the few surviving Koryo pieces protected by museum curators and private collectors in Korea and other countries over the centuries.

During the Koryo Dynasty, (935 -1392) Korea's master potters developed a lovely, translucent gray-green glaze called Celadon. The Korean royal court, Buddhist temple abbots, and well-to-do families commissioned the clay masters to produce Celadon teacups, teapots, bowls and vases.

In contrast to China and Japan, where pottery shapes tended to be simple and functional, Korea's ceramic artists played with the clay to produce whimsical shapes based on nature – pumpkins, bamboo, flower petals and even ducks, rabbits and lion-dogs.

Royal families in China imported Koryo Celadon ceramics because they loved the natural forms and could not create the same subtle glaze. Even today's master ceramicists have not figured out how potters were able to achieve that elusive beauty over 750 years ago.

Koryo Dynasty (12th/13th century) Celadon glazed incense burner with open-work round cover, lotus leaves and cute little bunnies.

During the Chosun Dynasty (1392-1910) Japanese forces invaded Korea. When they finally left in 1598 after a seven-year occupation, they took whole villages of potters with them. Back in Japan, these skilled artisans were supported by rich warlords and their work was the beginning of Japan's famous porcelain industry.

It wasn't just the fancy Celadon vases that impressed the Japanese. Surprisingly, they also preferred the ordinary, undecorated Korean rice bowls. During the 15th century Zen Buddhist monks in Japan discovered their beauty and imported them for their tea ceremonies. To the monks, these plain bowls represented the simple life lived by Buddha. Even Hidioshi, the Shogun of Japan, treasured a Korean peasant's rough rice bowl at his table.

Today, some of Korea's highly skilled old ceramics masters have been designated "Human Cultural Assets" by the government. ▣

19th century (Chosun Dynasty) white porcelain jar, 40 cm high, with longevity symbols: pine tree, deer, turtle, crane, funguses and clouds.

십 장 생

Ship Jang Seng
THE TEN LONGEVITY SYMBOLS

How many Ship Jang Seng *longevity symbols can you find?*

IN OLD KOREA, living to the age of 60 (five 12-year cycles of the Chinese zodiac) meant that you had lived a full life. A man could consider his life complete. He could stop shaving and grow a beard. He could retire and be supported in comfort by his sons. Long life and old age were blessings, rewards for working hard and raising a family.

So it is not surprising to find that ancient symbols representing "long life" have always been popular in Korea. Called *Ship Jang Seng*, the Ten Longevity Symbols are ten objects from nature that appear in decorations everywhere.

You may see Korean paintings include turtles, deer, or cranes to symbolize long life. You might also see a satin bedspread embroidered with the sun, clouds, and pine trees since they also represent long life. A ceramic vase might be decorated with images of mountains, rocks, and water – yes, they each represent long life.

The tenth symbol was a mythical wild edible fungus called *pulno-cho*, which means "longevity plant." According to legend, these mushroom-like plants are hard to find because only someone with a pure heart can see them. If you can spot one in the woods and eat it, you will never get old.

The Ten Longevity Symbols appear in Korean art through the ages. Few ancient paintings have survived the peninsula's rough history, but the ones seen today usually contain several of the long-life symbols; perhaps a deer beneath a pine tree beside a waterfall nibbling the odd-looking *pulno-cho* plant. A beautiful silk folding screen, used as a room divider or a wall decoration, might have all ten symbols scattered through a scenic landscape.

Who knows? Perhaps having a peaceful painting like this in your bedroom just might encourage your body to live longer. Old customs have staying power. Even today one can find these hopeful symbols almost everywhere in Korea.

무당 Mudang: THE SORCERESS

WHO DO YOU CALL when you think someone has put a curse on you? Or you're having trouble finding a job or a husband? Or your baby has a fever?

Traditionally, Korean people would summon a sorceress or shaman to heal the sick, to remove career obstacles, or to get one's life back on track.

The people of Korea have long believed in sorcery. Shamans claiming to have supernatural powers have practiced their arts since civilization began, acting as human links between this world and the spirit world.

In this ancient folk tradition, the shaman or sorceress is called a *mudang*. Usually a woman, her followers believe that she possesses mystical powers to communicate with the spirits of those who have passed away. She comes to the house where the problem is and performs a ritual. Dancing, chanting and jingling bells, the *mudang* enters a trance-like state and "channels" messages from beyond to find out what is causing the difficulty and fix it.

The shaman's ceremony is called a *mudang goot*. When the sound of gongs and drumming begins, neighbors hurry over to see the show. There is singing, dancing, and feasting. Buddhist sutras are recited, myths are recounted, and everyone watches as spirits of the dead supposedly take control of the sorceress and speak through her. The participants can expect to enjoy wit, laughter, and even a good cry. With her colorful costumes and dramatic gestures, the *mudang* provides entertainment as well as healing.

The practice of shamanism was repressed in Korea during the early 1900s and after the Korean War. As Christianity spread through the country, the old custom faded away even more. Today, however, the supernatural rituals are once again popular and seen as a unique aspect of Korean culture.

A mudang *performs a spiritual ceremony*

31

장승 Changsung: TOTEM COUPLE

A pair of changsung, *the totem couple, guard a village.*

AT ONE TIME, you would have seen them standing together, guarding the entrance to each village. Sometimes they marked the high point of a road or mountain pass near an ancient shrine to the local gods. Sometimes they just stood at the side of a country road as mileposts or distance markers. They were the totem couple, *changsung*.

The *changsung* were carved from logs and stood as crooked or as straight as the trees they once were. Planted along the path into the village to ward off wayward spirits, villagers saw the pair as much more than just lucky charms. They were the guardians of Heaven and Earth. Their origin goes back to early folk religion and echoes the symbolism of the yin-yang circle, harmony and balance in all things. Chinese characters painted onto their flattened fronts read "General of the World Above" for him and "General of the World Below" for her.

Passersby along the road might make a wish upon a stone and leave the stone at the feet of the Totem Couple. The wish could be for a safe journey, a happy marriage, or the birth of a son. Eventually, the pile of stones would grow and grow. Years later, long after the Totem Couple had rotted away, the pile of stones remained, creating a lasting good luck shrine.

More ambitious villages planted new Totem Couples with a ceremony each year. The resulting cluster of weathered Totem People, some old and some new, became a silent welcoming committee for anyone approaching the village.

It is hard to find these wooden Totem Couples in the Korean countryside any longer. You are more likely to find them in the cities newly carved and painted for the entertainment of tourists – a modern reminder of Korea's unique ancient culture. ▨